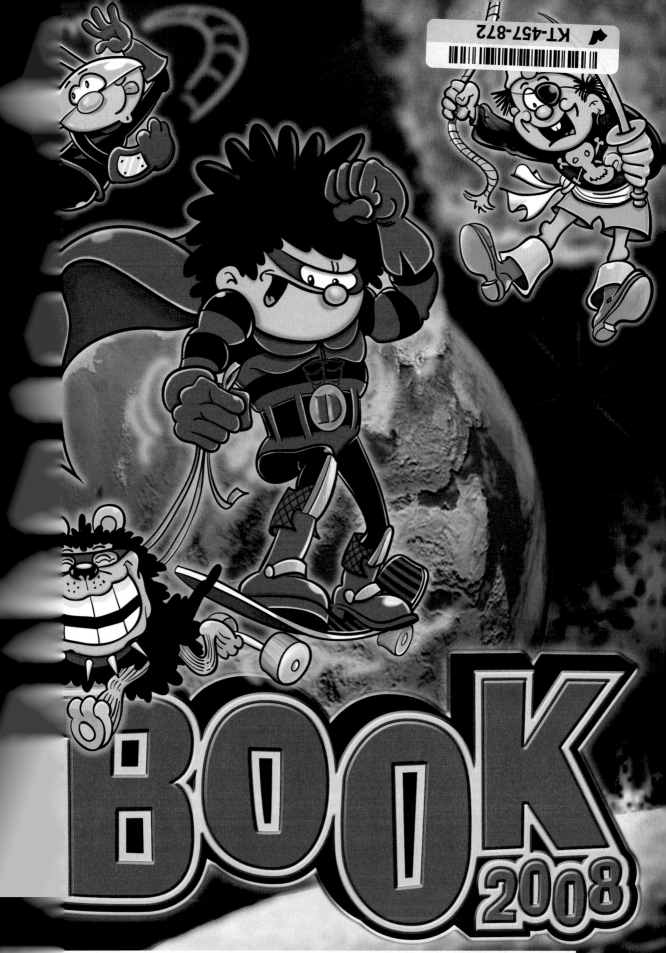

KT-457-872

BOOK 2008

Printed and Published in Great Britain by D. C. Thomson & Co., Ltd.,
185 Fleet Street, London, © D. C. Thomson & Co., Ltd., 2007.   ISBN 1 84535 319 3

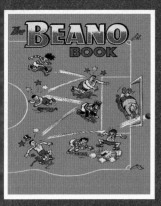

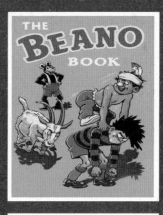
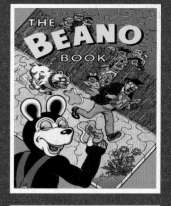

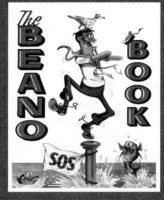
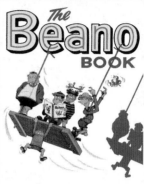

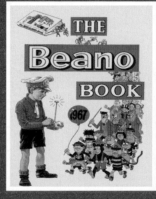
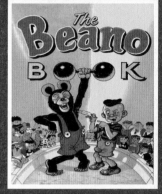

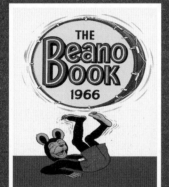
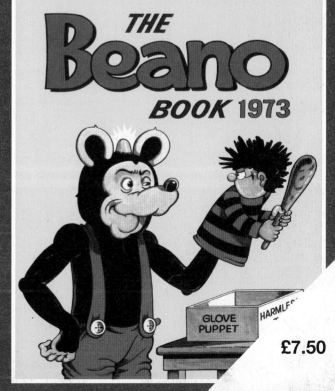
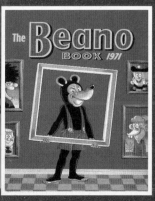
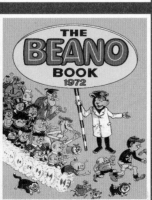

£7.50

RATZ-OOI-B

LES PRETEND'S MOVIE BLOCKBUSTERS!

ROGER THE DODGER IN: LIE ANOTHER DAY.

I'M DODGER, ROGER THE DODGER!

SUPER DOGS - CRIMINAL POSTIES BEWARE!

IS IT A BIRD? IS IT A PLANE?

NO, IT'S GNASHER AND GNIPPER!

Shortly...

THE RACE IS ABOUT TO START, BUT I'M NOT WORRIED!

SPLUNGE! SHLOP!

BECAUSE THAT LAST DODGE WORKED A TREAT! THAT LOT CAN HARDLY MOVE IN THEIR HEAVY, WET CLOTHES! I'VE GOT MORE DODGES WHEN THEY START TO CATCH UP TOO!

Later...

HMM! THEIR CLOTHES MUST BE DRYING OUT – HERE THEY COME!

AND HERE...

SQUIRT!

DAD'S OIL CAN

Rasher

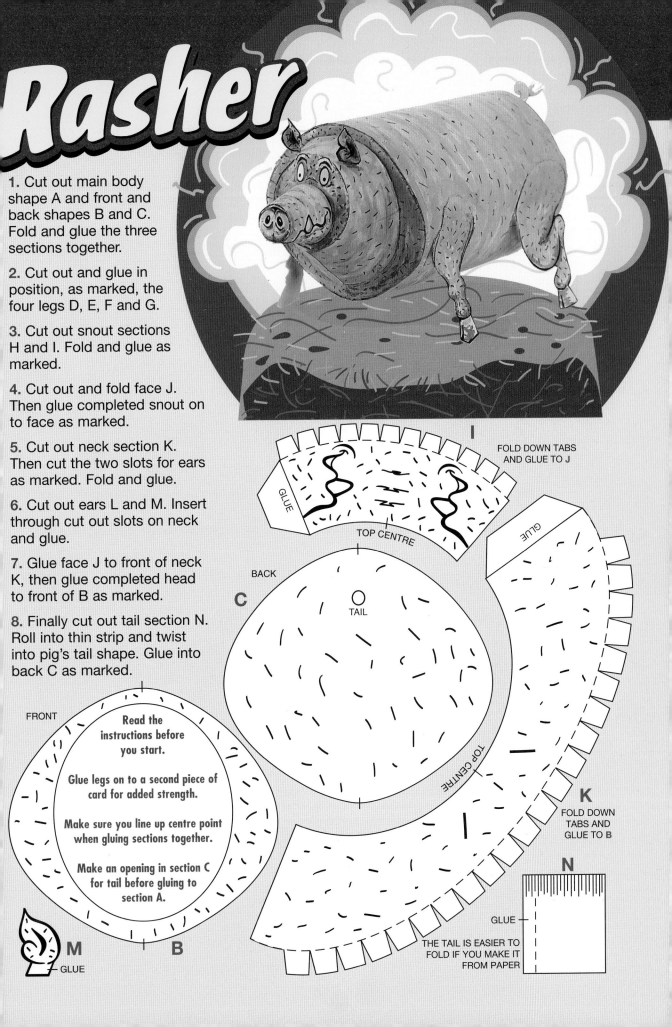

1. Cut out main body shape A and front and back shapes B and C. Fold and glue the three sections together.

2. Cut out and glue in position, as marked, the four legs D, E, F and G.

3. Cut out snout sections H and I. Fold and glue as marked.

4. Cut out and fold face J. Then glue completed snout on to face as marked.

5. Cut out neck section K. Then cut the two slots for ears as marked. Fold and glue.

6. Cut out ears L and M. Insert through cut out slots on neck and glue.

7. Glue face J to front of neck K, then glue completed head to front of B as marked.

8. Finally cut out tail section N. Roll into thin strip and twist into pig's tail shape. Glue into back C as marked.

I

FOLD DOWN TABS AND GLUE TO J

GLUE

TOP CENTRE

BACK

GLUE

C

O
TAIL

TOP CENTRE

FRONT

Read the instructions before you start.

Glue legs on to a second piece of card for added strength.

Make sure you line up centre point when gluing sections together.

Make an opening in section C for tail before gluing to section A.

K

FOLD DOWN TABS AND GLUE TO B

N

GLUE

THE TAIL IS EASIER TO FOLD IF YOU MAKE IT FROM PAPER

M

GLUE

B

Most people think burglars work at *night*, but they're wrong.

Most burglars come in the *day*, when folks are at work or at school.

See this bloke? He knows that *Neighbourhood Watch* doesn't work if the neighbours are all out.

He looks left.

He looks right.

He looks behind him.

What a shame he forgot to do one last thing...

...Look up!

GLERK!

WHO THE ...?

TWO GUESSES.

BILLY the CAT

CORRECT. YOU HAVE ONE GUESS LEFT.

in THE GENERAL

Part One

YOU CAN USE IT TO GUESS WHEN THE *POLICE* WILL COME TO GET YOU DOWN!

WILL IT BE *BEFORE* OR *AFTER* THOSE PIGEONS COME BACK TO RECLAIM THEIR FAVOURITE *POOPING SPOT?*

SPLAT!!

SORRY, DID *YOU* JUST SAY THAT?

EUGH! *THAT* SHOULD TEACH HIM CRIME DOESN'T PAY!

NICE *CRIME-FIGHTING*, BILLY.

THANK YOU.

YES. WHY? ARE YOU *SURPRISED* TO SEE ME WAY UP HERE ON THE ROOF?

N-NO. *THAT'S* NOT THE SURPRISING BIT.

YOU'RE A *TALKING CAT*, RIGHT? BUT HOW CAN YOU...?

WANT TO FIND OUT? *CHASE* ME!

COME BACK HERE!

SHEE-YEAH, COS THAT *ALWAYS* WORKS WITH CATS!

COULD THIS BE A FELINE *SUPER-POWER* I'VE NOT DISCOVERED BEFORE? *WOW* – I CAN TALK TO CATS!

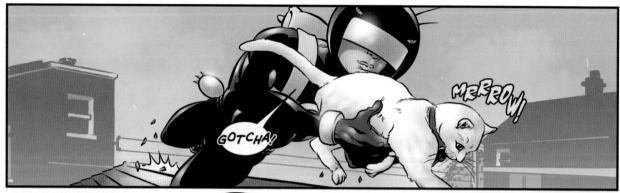

EESH!

SHOOSH

TA-DA! SURELY THE PERFECT TEN THIS TIME.

HMMM...

WELL...

COULD BE...

9.7 9.6 9.9

SPLOTCH!!

...BUT IT'S NOT – YOU FORGOT ABOUT HIS HAT.

SNARL!

FUME!

BELLOW!

SHE'S TAKING IT BETTER THAN I EXPECTED.

9.7 9.6 9.9

Nearby...

WATCH OUT! ESCAPED GORILLA!

GRRRNNN. GRUNT!

GORILL

CALAMITY JAMES

AND HIS PET - ALEXANDER LEMMING!

—TOM PATERSON—

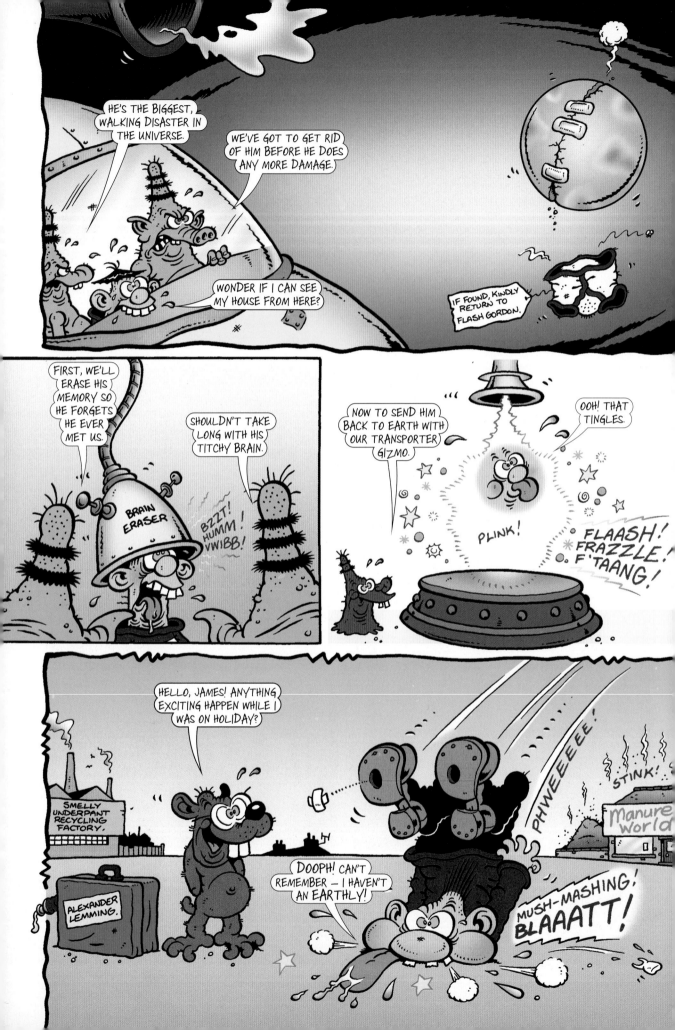

WGHMFTMWF

IK IK IK

EVER WONDERED WHAT'S GOING ON INSIDE PLUG'S HEAD AT A TIME LIKE THIS?

WELL, WONDER NO MORE!

LOOK!

PLUG HAS NUMSKULLS OF HIS VERY OWN! THEY'RE CALLED

PLUGSKULLS

EMERGENCY SUCTION! DON'T LET HIM DRIBBLE! REPEAT — STOP THE DRIBBLE!

WHAT ARE ALL THESE BUTTERFLIES DOING IN HIS TUM?

HOY, MOUTHY! WHAT HAPPENED? CAT GOT HIS TONGUE?

THINK OF SOME WORDS THEN, BRAIN-ACHE!

SLURP!

FLUTTER FLUTTER!

SHE'S A GIRL! WHAT CAN YOU SAY TO A GIRL?

CRANK UP THE 'THINGS TO SAY' MACHINE!

DID YOU SEE THE MATCH LAST NIGHT?

NO USE, SHE'S A GIRL!

DO YOU WANT A FIGHT?

NO GOOD, SEE ABOVE

AREN'T GIRLS STUPID?

OH, THIS IS USELESS!

②

③

④

And inside Plug?

PULL, BOYS, PULL!!

IT'S NO USE! THIS HEART IS ALL A-FLUTTER!

PLUG'S GONE SOFT IN THE HEAD!

MAYBE SHE'S A MIND-CONTROLLING MUTANT WHO'S SUCKED HIS BRAIN OUT!

SOMEONE MUST HAVE SUCKED HER BRAIN OUT!

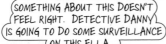

SOMETHING ABOUT THIS DOESN'T FEEL RIGHT. DETECTIVE DANNY IS GOING TO DO SOME SURVEILLANCE ON THIS ELLA ...

OKAY, SHE LIVES IN A NORMAL HOUSE, ON A NORMAL STREET.

G'NIGHT, ELLA.

G'NIGHT, PLUGGY WUGGY.

AND THEY HAVE A NORMAL LOUNGE, WITH NORMAL FURNITURE, AND A NORMAL TELLY.

AND, HELLO, SOMEONE'S COMING IN —

HELLO, DADDY.

HELLO, ELLA DEAR.

OH, NO! OH, MY SAINTED AUNTS! AND MY SAINTED UNCLES! AND ALL MY SAINTED COUSINS!! IT CAN'T BE!!!

PLUG IS GOING OUT WITH —

BABY-FACE FINLAYSON'S DAUGHTER!

BIB

5

BABY-FACE FINLAYSON'S DAUGHTER?

YES!

NO SOFTIES

PLUG'S GIRLFRIEND IS BABY-FACE FINLAYSON'S DAUGHTER!

HOY! NO PEEKING!

BABY-FACE FINLAYSON'S DAUGHTER?

YES!

BABY-FACE FINLAYSON THE GANGSTER?

YES!

THE SAME BABY-FACE FINLAYSON WHO ONCE STOLE OUR SCHOOL BY CHEATING AT TIDDLYWINKS?

THE VERY SAME.

THE BABY-FACE FINLAYSON WHO ONCE STOLE ALL HANK'S HOT ROD COW MEMORABILIA AND THEN—

OKAY! WE KNOW WHO HE IS ALREADY!

BUT IF ELLA'S HIS DAUGHTER SHE'S BOUND TO BE EVIL TOO!

NOT NECESSARILY.

I MEAN NONE OF US ARE LIKE OUR MUMS AND DADS, ARE WE?

NO. WE'RE COMPLETELY DIFF—

FATTY! I BROUGHT YOU SOME SANDWICHES COS I THOUGHT YOU MIGHT BE HUNGRY. SORRY, I ATE HALF ON THE WAY!

WE'RE COMPLETELY DIFF—

6

⑦

Inside Plug's head –

STOP ALL THESE SOFT, GOOEY THOUGHTS! THEY'RE CLOGGING UP HIS NOSE!

LOVEY DOVEYNESS

SLOPPY SENTIMENTS

SWEET NOTHINGS

TREACLE TALK

AND INSIDE ELLA'S HEAD (OH YES, SHE HAS NUMSKULLS TOO)

SO, HE'S A BOY, HE SMELLS, GET USED TO IT!

BRIDGET JONES DIARY

IT'S NO GOOD BEING SUBTLE! WE HAVE TO CONFRONT THEM WITH THE TRUTH!

OOH, THIS'LL BE PAINFUL!

PLUG! ELLA! LISTEN UP, LOVEBIRDS!

YES?

CAN WE HELP?

YOU CAN'T GO OUT WITH HER 'COS SHE IS BABY-FACE FINLAYSON'S DAUGHTER!

WHAT?

LOOK – WE HAVE VIDEO EVIDENCE!

HELLO ELLA.

HELLO DAD.

KEVF DVD PLAYERS

B–B–BUT IF THIS IS TRUE –

9

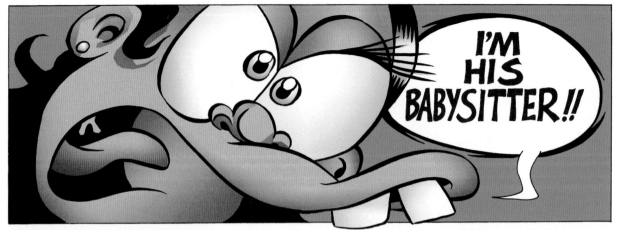

I'M HIS BABYSITTER!!

CLICK WHIRR

GRIND

CHURN

GIMME A K GIMME AN E GIMME AN AV & AN F

UH-OH! WHAT'S GOING ON INSIDE DANNY'S BRAIN?

HELP HIM PUT TWO & TWO TOGETHER, BEFORE HE EXPLODES!

GRIND

YES! HE'S A BABY! IDIOT!

DON'T JUMP!

PLUG! CAN YOU HEAR US?

CAN YOU LOT KEEP THE NOISE DOWN? I'M TRYING TO HAVE A CRY OVER HERE.

HOT ROD CLAY

PLUG! YOU'RE SAFE! HOORAY!

THEN WHO'S THAT UP ON THE ROOF?

THAT'S A SCULPTURE ELLA MADE OF ME. WE THOUGHT IT WOULD MAKE A GOOD SCARECROW.

IT'S A BIT FRAGILE, THOUGH, I HOPE NO-ONE TOUCHES IT.

STAND BACK TEACH — I'M GOING IN!

15

NO, WE CAN'T. I WAS ONLY HERE FOR A SHORT WHILE. I MOVE TO A NEW SCHOOL TOMORROW.

NO WORRIES. I'LL POP OVER AND A VISIT.

WHERE IS THIS NEW SCHOOL?

AMERICA.

OS ORDINARY SERVILE MAP OF BEANOTOWN

— ROAD
— PATH
— WALL
— RIVER
— CREASE
— BIT OF BIRO

BOO HOO HOO!

OH COME ON! WE JUST RE-FILLED THOSE TEAR DUCTS!

BUT VERY SOON EVERYTHING GETS BACK TO NORMAL ...

HEY, PLUG? REMEMBER WHEN YOU HAD A GIRLFRIEND?

NO.

KEEP OFF THE GRASS

I MEAN IT! YOU LITTLE

I'LL TELL YOU WHAT THOUGH SPOTTY. THAT NEW GIRL FANCIES YOU!

HO HO! PULL THE OTHER—

GULP!

RECEPTION

THE DAVY SUTHERLAND ART ROOM

AND INSIDE SPOTTY..?

OH NO! HERE WE GO! ALL SYSTEMS READY FOR LURVE!

THE END

WHOOOSH!

BUT MY METAL CHUM CAN STEAM THE PAPER OFF . . .

Once the paper's removed —

READY, WIMPBOT?

YES, MASTER.

TEN SECONDS SHOULD DO IT.

WHOOOSH!

SOME LOVELY STEAMED FISH FOR FLUFFY.

NOW, INTO THE SOFTY CHALET.

HEE, HEE! DENNIS'S KNEES HAVE RECOVERED.

GRUMP.

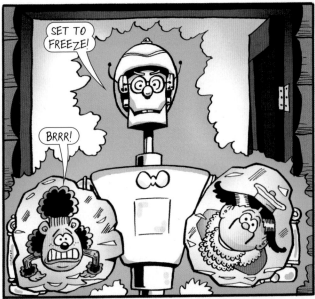

TO BE CONTINUED

BEANO BRAI

WHO'S MISSING?

Can you spot which character is missing fr

MAGNET MAYHEM

Oops! Bea's been having fun rearranging the message Mum left for Dennis on the fridge. Can you unmuddle it before Dennis gets grounded for not doing what he's told!

LANCE
OYUR
MOOR

EENY MEANY MINI MO!

Only two of these pictures of Roger are identical. Can you suss out which two?

BAFFLERS!

...ese piccies?

SPOT THE SPOTS!!
Can you count how many zits Spotty has today?

DiG 'EM UP!
Gnasher and Gnipper have buried BONES all over these pages! Can you spot them all?

READ ALL ABOUT iT
Can you work out which characters these newspaper headlines are dishing the dirt on?

BEANO times
James
Sued over Paint Disaster
(Exclusive pictures of the Calamity on page 5)
①

BEANO times
Mini Bank Robber
Foiled
(The minx was caught red handed!)
②

BEANO times
Speed Cameras Not Fast Enough to Catch Boy
(The culprit whizzed by at 3pm Friday, witnesses sought by police)
③

Answers: Who's Missing? - 1 Dennis' Dad, 2 Gnipper, 3 Fatty, 4 Ivy, Spot the Spots - 20, Dig 'Em Up - there are 10 bones hidden.
Read All About It - 1 Calamity James, 2 Minnie the Minx, 3 Billy Whizz, Magnet Mayhem - Clean Your Room, Eeny Meany Mini Mo – 3 and 6

High above the farm —

DEREK the SHEEP

PAAARRP!!!

Watcha, readers! Farmer Jack has stuck us on the side of a mountain again!

So I like to slap on my 'Lederhosen'* and give my mad Swiss 'Alpenhorn' a good Parp!

*Lederhosen— the loopy trousers as worn by all Swiss people. Probably.

YODEL-AY....
YODEL-AY....

EEE-HEEE!!

Flippin' 'eck!

And Cecil likes to practise his yodelling.

Watcha readers.

Lederhosen for little bees

Watch this ...

YODEL-AY EEHEEE!

Check out the echo on that!

..... Yodel-ay eehee...

Pah! Any fool can make an echo!

THEY'RE SO SOFT WHEN YOU'RE LANDING. AND I KNOW ALL THEIR NAMES – LIONS, SEALS, SNAKES.

NNYAH! KNOW YOUR ANMALS, EH, IVY. BET YOU DON'T KNOW ANY ANIMALS THAT BEGIN WITH 'N'.

MR. SOFTY, I'M AN ANIMAL EXPERT.

LET ME THINK, LET ME THINK, LET ME ... GOTTIT!

I'VE GOT ONE, MR SOFT PERSON! NELLYPHANT!

DON'T BE SUCH A SILLY LITTLE GIRL. ELEPHANT STARTS WITH AN 'E'.

ROTTON OLD SOFTY. JUST COS HE CAN SPELL. GULP! SOB!

SLAM!

I'LL SHOW HIM. I'LL FIND SOME BRILLIANT ANIMALS THAT START WITH AN 'N'!

FOUND ONE FOUND ONE ALREADY!

ODD LITTLE GIRL.

I'M NEVER GOING TO GET THIS RIGHT AND SHOW THE SOFTY.

STOMP!

But later –

I'VE GOT AN ANIMAL STARTING WITH 'N'.

DO YOU NOW? WHAT IS IT PRAY TELL? A NARWHAL?

HAH! THAT MUTT? GNIPPER DOESN'T START WITH AN 'N'.

NOPE. BUT HE STARTS WITH A ...

GNNN...

N–N–N–NO! H–HELP! CALL HIM ORF!

GNIP!

THAT SOFTY STARTED WITH AN 'N'!

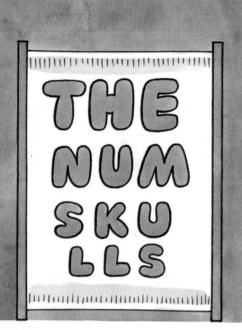

THE NUM SKU LLS

Edd Case is the Numskulls' boy —

SPIN! SPIN!

EYE DEPT.

OH, NO! EDD'S EYES ARE TOTALLY OUT OF CONTROL WITHOUT BLINKY!

COOL!

Enter Edd's Mum —

YOU'RE GOING TO THE OPTICIAN'S EDD. WE MUST DO SOMETHING ABOUT THOSE EYES OF YOURS.

DRAG!

I FEEL SICK.

EDD DOESN'T NEED EXPENSIVE SPECS. WE JUST NEED BLINKY TO GET BACK IN CONTROL OF EDD'S EYEBALLS.

YEAH! BLINKY!

And so —

TAKE A SEAT, YOUNG SIR.

I. LIDD OPTICIAN

OPTICIAN

GROGGY.

The 10 Silliest Excuses For Being Late For School!

These excuses were tried out on unsuspecting teachers. Surprisingly they didn't buy them!

(1) I fell in a huge puddle and had to wait for my clothes to dry out.

(2) Didn't you feel the earthquake?

(3) I was late for class because I was fighting with a kid who said that you weren't the best teacher in the world.

(4) I was here on time... I was just invisible. I had to go back to my lab. To get the visibility serum.

(5) It's my alarm clock's fault. It's never been the same since I hit it with that sledgehammer.

(6) I was stuck in the bathroom without any loo paper!

(7) Sorry I was late. The bell rang before I got here!

(8) Duh! I was trying to be fashionably late!

(9) We have a really old toaster that just takes ages to warm up in the mornings.

(10) My foot fell asleep and I didn't want to wake it up.

YOU AND YOUR *MINI MANIACS* HAVE *SHOT* AT ME! *BOMBED* ME! *ZAPPED* ME! CUT MY SUIT TO *RIBBONS* AND *DENTED* MY BEST HELMET!

WHAT'S YOUR *GAME*, JUMBO? COME ON, SPEAK UP! *WHAT - IS - YOUR...?*

ARE YOU *CRYING?*

DON'T CRY. I DON'T *GET* THIS. WHAT'S *WRONG* WITH YOU?

LET ME GO-O-OH. WH-WHY... *SNIFF* ...WHY ARE YOU *SHOUTING* AT ME?

WHY AM I *SHOUTING?* WHICH BIT OF *"YOU TRIED TO KILL ME"* DON'T YOU UNDERSTAND?

N-NO, I *SNIFF* DIDN'T.

I'M *GENERAL JUMBO.* I'M A *GOOD* BOY.

I TRIED TO *TELL* YOU THAT. *HERE...* HAVE YOUR *WRIST* THING.

THANKS BILLY. SEE, I ONLY EVER DO *GOOD* STUFF. HELPING OLD LADIES ACROSS THE ROAD, RESCUING CATS FROM TREES, THAT SORT OF THING.

I'VE BEEN DOING IT FOR *YEARS.*

CLICK

EVERYBODY KNOWS ME. I'VE ALWAYS BEEN...

...A TOTAL *WIMP!*

BUT NOT ANY LONGER!

WAIT! YOU WERE *GOOD* A SECOND AGO!

SORRY, I DON'T KNOW WHAT CAME OVER ME!

BUT I THINK *I* DO. IF I CAN JUST OUTFOX THESE *MINI MISSILES!*

THIS WAY, BOMB-BOYS! COME AND *GET* ME!

OOPS, SHOELACE.

FD-DOOM!

SP-DAAASH!

NO!! FRIENDLY FIRE!!!

YOU'LL *PAY* FOR THAT, YOU *POINTY-EARED...*

S W I P E !

oh.

W-WHAT *HAPPENED* BILLY?

THIS DID. SOMEONE'S *TAMPERED* WITH YOUR *WRIST CONTROL.*

ARE THOSE *TINY ELECTRODES* USUALLY THERE?

N-NO.

THOUGHT NOT. THEY'RE SENDING SOME KIND OF *MIND-CONTROLLING* SIGNAL THROUGH YOUR *WRIST* TO YOUR *BRAIN.*

WHO COULD *DO* SUCH A THING?

I DON'T KNOW. BUT TILL WE FIND OUT, WE'D BEST LEAVE YOUR TROOPS *DE-ACTIVATED.*

LANCE CORPORAL JONES – DISMISSED.

INTO THE BOX.

CLICK

SERGEANT-MAJOR WILSON – DISMISSED.

INTO THE BOX.

DO YOU *HAVE* TO DO THAT? IT'S *WEIRD.*

CLICK

PRIVATE PIKE – DISMISSED.

INTO THE BOX.

CLICK

I don't want to go into the box.

Are Jumbo's soldiers rebelling? Find out in the thrilling conclusion!

End of Part Two

FREDDIE FEAR

MUM? HOW COME I'VE NEVER DONE ANYTHING NORMAL?

NORMAL?

YEAH. NORMAL. I'VE NEVER EVEN BEEN ON A TRAIN.

BUT, FREDDIE. BROOMSTICKS ARE FASTER, QUIETER, MORE FUEL EFFI . . .

A TRAIN, MUM!

OK, A TRAIN YOU WANT AND TRAIN YOU'LL GET.

BASH STREET KIDS PUT TO THE TEST!

Oh dear! Teach isn't looking very chuffed with the Bash Street Kids' test papers! No wonder - check out what the rascals have written!

Name: Smiffy

(1) Which Queen reigned the longest? ✗
Queen Victoria She sat on a thorn for 63 years!

(2) How did Benjamin Franklin first produce electricity? ✗
By rubbing a cat's fur backwards.

(3) What is the answer? ✗
1 + 1 = 11

(4) How many feet are in a furlong? ✗
Depends on how many feet the furlong ate for breakie that day.

(5) Find x ✗
Here it is
x
3cm
4cm

(6) Write the letters of the alphabet. ✗
A-Z ta da!

(7) How many hours are in a day? ✗
Don't know. Cuthbert's arm is blocking his paper. Whatever he wrote on his sheet.

Name: Danny

(1) What is the capital of France? ✗
This information is only available on a "need-to-know" basis. Please request military clearance before asking this question again.

(2) What language do they speak in China? ✗
Refer to question 1. Please show identification when requesting TOP SECRET data again. Authorized personnel only!

(3) Clogs come from which country? ✗
I don't know and I don't care but whoever invented them should be given a visit from the fashion police.

(4) If you were standing next to the Leaning Tower of Pisa where would you be? ✗
Running like Billy Whiz away from the death trap! They should knock it down, that's dangerous, man.

(5) The boomerang originated where? ✗
Look what's with all the questions? General Blythe says I should get an A. So listen up 'cos he has an army that'll kick your butt if you don't do as he says!

(6) Which continent is Germany on? ✗
Ok wise guy, you asked for it.

THIS PAPER WILL SELF DESTRUCT IN 10 SECONDS.
10, 9, 8, 7, 6.....

WARNING

WARNING

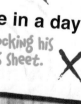

RUBB

Name: *Cuthbert*

(1) When was the first World War?
What an excellent question, it was 1914-1918 You are the bestest teacher in the world and so clever, too! xxx ✓

(2) What colour do you get if you mix together red and yellow?
Orange, it's my favourite colour. What's yours? ✓

(3) What would you like to be when you grow up?
A teacher just like you! ✓

(4) When is the Queen's birthday?
13 days after yours. Did you like the flowers I sent you? ✓

(5) What is the internet?
Full of websites about cool stuff. I have one all about you! We have 3 members and it's called My Teacher is the Greatest.com! ✓

(6) Who invented the telephone?
Alexander Graham Bell. Will you be my best friend? Call me! ✓

Name: FATTY

(1) You have 20 pence and you buy an apple that costs 10p and an orange that costs 5p. What would you be left with?
A RUMBLING TUMMY! ✗

(2) Name the four seasons.
SALT, PEPPER, VINEGAR AND MUSTARD. ALL VERY TASTY ON CHIPS. MMMM... ✗

(3) What happens to your body when you age?
WHEN YOU GET OLD, SO DO YOUR BOWELS AND YOU GET INTERCONTINENTAL. ✗

(4) What do vegetarians eat?
ANYTHING A RABBIT DOES. ✗

(5) What are mushrooms?
THEY GROW IN WET PLACES SO THEY LOOK LIKE UMBRELLAS. THEY ALSO TASTE GOOD ON PIZZA. ✗

(6) Where was the battle of Waterloo?
I HAVE AN RSI (THUMB STRAIN) FROM PLAYING PLAYSTATION LAST NIGHT SO I'LL HAVE TO SKIP THIS QUESTION AND REST. ✗

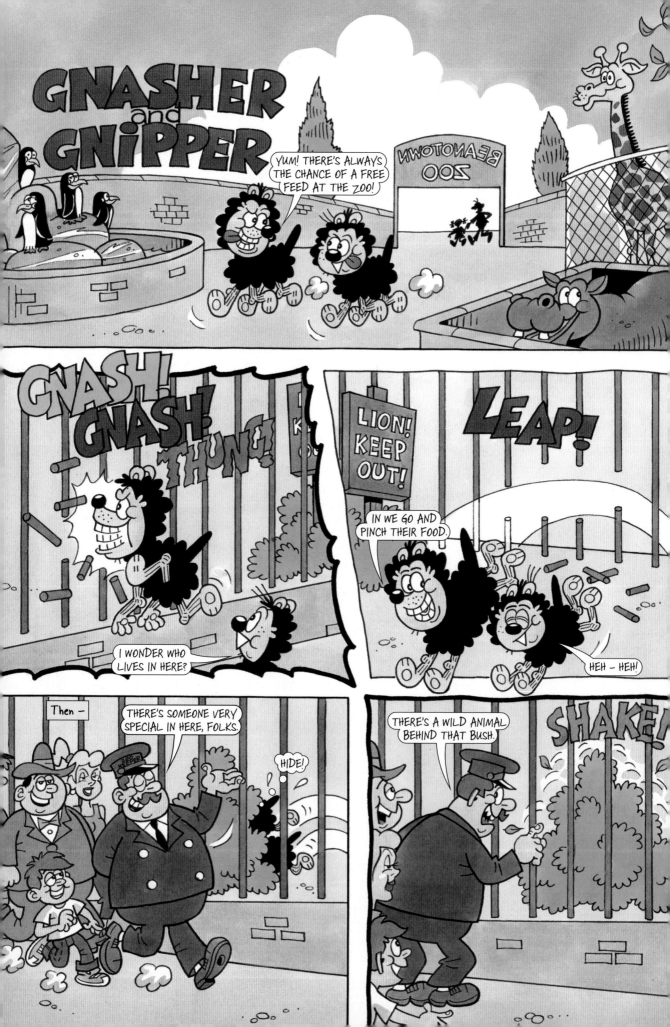

WELL, CUTHBERT, DEAR BOY, YOU'LL BE DELIGHTED TO KNOW I DID WRITE A CHILDREN'S BOOK ONCE. DIDN'T SHOW IT TO ANYONE, OF COURSE.

OH, SIR! I WOULD DEARLY LOVE TO READ IT. OR HEAR YOU READ IT — THAT WOULD BE EVEN BETTER!

WHAT AN EXCELLENT TEACHER'S PET YOU ARE, CUTHBERT.

OH, SO WOULD WE SIR!

Seconds later —

I'VE JUST NIPPED HOME TO FETCH MY MASTERPIECE, ER, — BOOK.

HARUMPH! I'LL JUST PREPARE MY VOCAL CHORDS.

RIGHT, NO LAUGHING, HOWEVER HARD IT IS TO KEEP A STRAIGHT FACE.

'THE STORY OF REACHER', PART ONE.

LONG AWAY, AND FAR AGO THERE LIVED A BRAVE AND HANDSOME LAD CALLED REACHER.

STOP IT YOU LOT!

BUT IT'S SO BAD!

THE LAD WAS CALLED REACHER, BECAUSE HE ALWAYS REACHED OUT TO NATURE.

OH, HO! HO! HO! I'M SORRY, DANNY, BUT I JUST CAN'T HELP IT!

REACHER LONGED TO WIN THE HAND OF ELIVE, THE BAKER'S, ER, BEAUTIFUL DAUGHTER.

THESE DEAD FLIES WILL LOOK LIKE RAISINS IN THE CAKE.

WAIL! WHAT A LOVELY STORY.

SMIFFY'S GOT IT WRONG AGAIN.

AT THE OUTSIDE OF REACHER'S TOWN WAS CASTLE DREAD, WHERE THE DREADMASTER LIVED. HE WAS A VILLAINOUS VILLAIN.

THE DREADMASTER LED A GROUP OF WICKED URCHINS, CALLED THE NIDS.

WAIT A MINUTE. THIS STORY'S ALL ABOUT YOU BEING THE BRAVE HERO, AND US BEING A BUNCH OF LITTLE BADDIES.

ALL THE CHARACTERS ARE FICTICIOUS AND BEAR NO RESEMBLANCE TO PEOPLE LIVING OR . . .

I'LL BUY THIS BOOK!

A FAN!

NO! JANITOR HAD RUN OUT OF COAL FOR THE CENTRAL HEATING!

HEAT

POP!

SOB! MY DREAMS OF FAME AND RICHES. UP IN SMOKE.

ROGER the DODGER

DODGE DAY

Oh, no! It's advanced long division theoretical geography class this morning. Can you help Roger dodge out of school without getting caught?

To avoid cutting up your annual, photocopy or scan the counters below. Then stick them to card, carefully cut them out and stick them back to back, folding the bottom tab so that they stand up. Use a die to race Roger home without getting caught.

GET DODGING!

1 2

BIKE SHED

GULP!

12 Oh no! Head's seen you! Hide in the bike shed. MISS A GO

13

15 ARGHHH! You've been caught by Teacher! BACK TO CLASS

14

18

16

17 BLAM! Your bike has a puncture. Take the long way on foot. Back to SPACE 6

DENNIS THE MENACE VERSUS THE WIMPBOT

PART THREE

GROAN. MENACING'S A THING OF THE PAST THANKS TO WALTER'S WIMPBOT. ONLY GOOD THING IS, THE METAL MANIAC HAS FORGOTTEN ABOUT ME AND GNASHER.

COME AND HAVE A LOOK AT THIS.

BEANOTOWN UNITED V DANDYTOWNCLOGGERS

CANCELLED

BALLET. SUPER.

LOOK WHAT THE WIMPBOT'S MADE THESE TOUGH FOOTBALLERS DO.

. . . AND, AS FOR THE BOXERS . . .

BEANO TOWN GYM

. . . THEY'VE HAD TO EMBROIDER THE CANVAS. POOR GUYS.

AND IT'S ALL BECAUSE IF YOU TRY TO STAND UP TO THE WIMPBOT . . .

I'VE HAD ENOUGH OF THIS!

FOOLISH HUMAN. YOU CANNOT THREATEN THE WIMPBOT.

ZZZZAP!

HE'LL BE SOFTYFIED . I CAN'T BEAR TO LOOK.

THAT'S IT. I'M GOING TO HAVE TO DO SOMETHING REALLY DRASTIC . . .

. . . STUDY.

TOUGH SCIENCE

SWOOON!

NORMALLY, I DON'T READ BOOKS LIKE THIS, BUT SINCE IT'S TOUGH ...

YAWN. STUDYING. I DON'T KNOW WHAT WALTER SEES IN IT . . .

In the morning —

AT LAST — I'M READY FOR THAT WIMPBOT.

SLAM!

NO, YOU DON'T!

DENNIS. A VOICE FROM THE PAST!

POF!

FOOL. DEMENACEIVATE HIM AGAIN, WIMPY.

OH, NO. HE'S GOT ME ALREADY.

DUH!

BZZZZZZ!

ZZZZPFF!

NOW TO USE MY NEW FOUND KNOWLEDGE...

TOOLS

HE'S DISTRACTED.

SHOULD I HAVE DENNIS THROWN IN PERFUME...

CUT THIS WIRE. REVERSE THIS CIRCUIT.

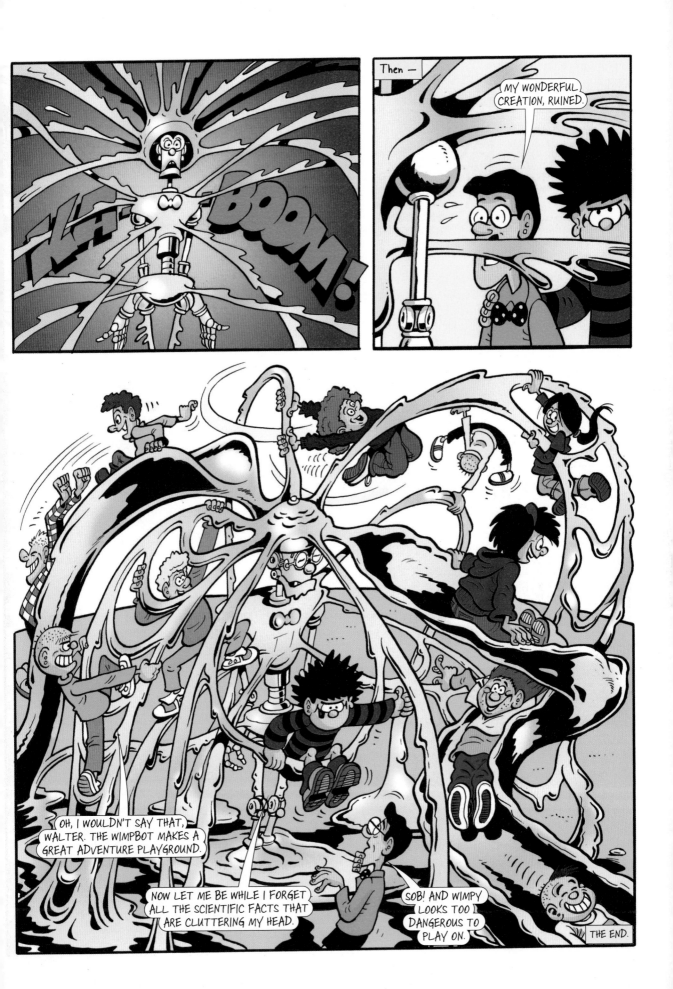

Confuse Santa in 10 easy steps

Have you been a Menace all year and are sure the only prezzies you'll be getting off Mr Claus at Xmas will be a pack of new pants and a tangerine? Well here's how to get your own back - Dennis style!

1 Turn your living room into a workshop. Have people dressed as elves making toys. When he comes down the chimney, sneer and say, "What's up? Afraid of a bit of competition are we?"

2 Before you go to bed leave a Bull beside the tree. You think a red flag makes 'em mad, well see what a red Santa outfit can do!

3 Instead of biscuits and milk leave a salad and diet book with a note saying you think he ought to lose some pork.

4 While he's in the house sneak out to his sledge and leave a speeding ticket.

5 Set a booby trap to capture Santa, keep him prisoner and steal all the presents.

6 Hack into his naughty and nice lists and make some major adjustments.

7 Empty your house of everything and when he arrives walk in dressed as a policeman and say "Ha! They always return to the scene of a crime, you're under arrest, beardy!"

8 Wait for him at the bottom of the chimney dressed in full Santa rig out and angrily accuse him of being an impostor.

9 Leave a note saying you've moved house. Attach a map with unclear, smudged and unreadable directions.

10 Wear a giant tree costume with a sign attached that says "Vicious Man-eating Tree - Beware!" As soon as he gets his foot in the door start thrashing about making scary noises and chase him back up that chimney.

Only joking, Santa. You're number one in our book.

BILLY the CAT & GENERAL JUMBO ★ in THE GENERAL Part Three

General Jumbo is no longer acting evil, but one of his soldiers is now refusing to co-operate!

P-PARDON?

I don't want to go into the box.

GET INTO THE BOX! You've de-activated them, right?

UH-HUH.

I don't want to go into the box.

OH YEAH? AND WHO ARE YOU, ALL OF A SUDDEN?

I'm your worst nightmare.

I'm the toy soldier who mutinied!

HOW CAN YOU MUTINY? YOU'RE MADE OF PLASTIC. I HELPED MAKE YOU.

YEAH, READ MY WHISKERS — YOU ARE A TOY!

Really? and can a toy do...

...this?

F-DOOOMPH!

FZZZZZ.ZZZAP!

TROOOOONCH!!

CAT-LEAP!

THAT IS ME OFFICIALLY DOWN TO *EIGHT LIVES*. SO, WHAT'S THIS ABOUT A LEARNING CHIP?

IT'S A PROGRAM THE *PROFESSOR* INVENTED. A SORT OF *ARTIFICIAL INTELLIGENCE* TO HELP THE TOYS *LEARN FOR THEMSELVES*.

WE WERE TESTING IT OUT IN *PRIVATE PIKE*.

I GUESS THIS MEANS IT *WORKS*.

YOU MEAN THAT *LUMP OF PLASTIC* CAN *THINK*?

WITH *PIKE* AND HIS *LEARNING CHIP* FRAZZLED ALL HIS *POWERS* HAVE GONE.

YOU'RE RIGHT.

ALTHOUGH, JUST TO BE ON THE *SAFE* SIDE...

TAKE THAT! AND THAT! AND THAT! AND THAT!

SMASH! CRUNCH! DESTROY! SPIFFLICATE! CRASH!

I WAS *GOING* TO SAY YOU COULD TAKE HIS *BATTERIES* OUT.

YES. THAT WOULD WORK TOO.

SO, WILL YOU AND THE PROFESSOR BE DOING ANY *MORE* WITH THIS *LEARNING CHIP?*

I DON'T *THINK* SO, BILLY.

THAT KIND OF THING'S TOO *SCARY* FOR ME. I'M GOING BACK TO HELPING *LITTLE OLD LADIES* ACROSS THE *STREET.*

AND IF YOU EVER WANT *RESCUING* FROM A *TREE...?*

I'LL BEAR IT IN MIND... THANKS.

I LOVE A *HAPPY ENDING,* DON'T YOU?

The End?

—TOM PATERSON—

FROM BEANOTOWN WITH LOVE

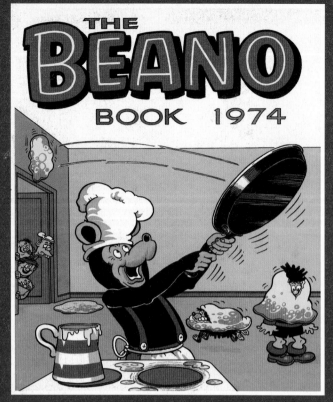

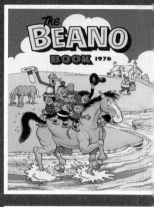

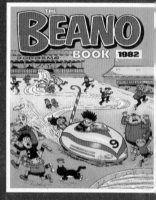
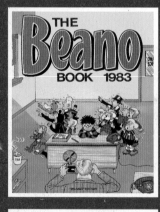
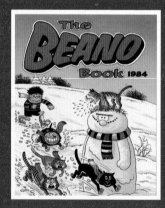
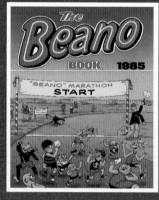
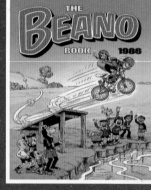

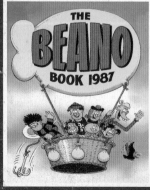
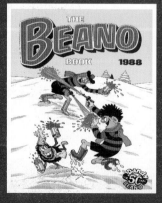
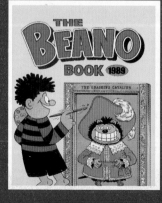
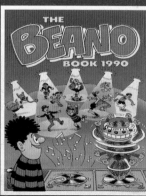